A Family in Pakistan

LIBRARY OF CONGRESS CATALOGING IN PUBLICATION DATA

Scarsbrook, Ailsa.
  A family in Pakistan.

  Rev. ed. of: Pakistani village. 1979.
  Summary: Presents the life of fourteen-year-old
Assim in a village in northern Pakistan.
  1. Pakistan—Social life and customs—Juvenile
literature. 2. Pakistan—Description and travel—
Juvenile literature. [1. Pakistan—Social life and
customs] I. Scarsbrook, Alan. II. Title.
DS379.S33 1985   954.9'1   85-6886
ISBN 0-8225-1662-4 (lib. bdg.)

Manufactured in the United States of America

2 3 4 5 6 7 8 9 10 95 94 93 92 91 90 89 88 87 86

A Family in Pakistan

Ailsa and Alan Scarsbrook

Lerner Publications Company · Minneapolis

Assim Mahmood lives with his mother, father, and two sisters in the village of Dhamial, three miles (five kilometers) from the nearby city of Rawalpindi in northern Pakistan.

Assim is 14 and goes to a boys' school in Rawalpindi. Each morning he gets up early to ride his bicycle into the city. He studies hard because he wants to earn good grades and be accepted at the military college at Murree. Assim would like to be an army officer. His father was once a soldier.

Assim's younger sister, Teybah, goes to the girls' school in Dhamial. His older sister, Shahida, stays at home to help their mother with the house.

Assim's father farms some land in the village. Many men work in the fields around Dhamial, growing corn, wheat, and vegetables and taking care of their goats, oxen, and buffalo. Some men, like the tailor Mr. Sabir, go to work in Rawalpindi every day.

Most houses in Dhamial are one-story buildings made of brick and sometimes covered with a hard, baked clay. The houses have flat roofs and wooden doors and window shutters. The window shutters are closed to keep out the hot sun. This makes the rooms dark inside but helps to keep them cool.

Dhamial has four mosques, or temples, where people pray. The village also has a mill, some stores, two schools, and a village council meeting house. There are several wells for water.

Many of the village streets are narrow and winding.
The children in Dhamial can play in them without having
to bother about any traffic.

Assim lives in one of the bigger houses of the village.
On the ground floor is a courtyard surrounded by a dining
room, living room, and kitchen.

Upstairs, there are several bedrooms, a bathroom, and
a balcony. Assim often sleeps out on the balcony or on
the roof during hot summer nights.

Assim's mother cooks the meals on a charcoal fire. Shahida helps prepare the food. A typical dinner includes lamb or beef with rice, potatoes, vegetables, and *chapattis*, a flat round bread. After dinner, they eat fruit and drink tea.

Assim's mother makes her own clothes on the sewing machine. Pakistani women and girls wear a *dupatta* (scarf), *kamiz* (tunic), and *shalwar* (slacks). Assim's mother even weaves the *nara* (belt) for her *shalwar* herself.

Assim's family is Muslim. They pray to Allah, or God, five times a day and read the Koran, their holy book. Assim and his father go to the village mosque to pray. Assim's grandmother says her prayers at home, facing toward Mecca.

During the holy month of Ramadan, Assim's parents fast. They do not eat or drink anything between sunrise and sunset. At the end of Ramadan, the family celebrates the festival of Eid. They have a feast, put on new clothes, and visit friends.

These village women are bringing water home from the well. Between their heads and the heavy jars is a cloth ring which helps keep the jars balanced. Because the jars are made of clay, the water in them stays cool.

The well is powered by a pair of oxen, which are blindfolded and made to walk around in a circle, turning the wooden wheels. The wheels drive a chain of buckets.

The buckets dip into the water deep down in the well and are then lifted up over the wheel at the top. There the water spills out into a trough. In some villages, the wells are operated with electric pumps.

Most of Pakistan has very little rain. The farmers living on the Punjab plain, like Assim's father, depend on a huge system of irrigation canals for water. These canals lead from the Indus River and its tributaries. Without this water, the farmers could not grow their crops.

In other villages, the irrigation channels lead from wells instead of directly from the river.

In Dhamial, most farmers till their land with a wooden plow pulled by oxen. Tractors are very expensive, and only a few farmers can afford one.

In April or May, the farmers harvest the wheat. First they cut it and lay it down on the flat ground. Then they lead the oxen around in a circle over it. The oxen trample the wheat until it becomes a heap of crushed straw, husks, and grain.

Next the farmers toss the wheat into the air with wooden forks. The wind blows away the chaff (straw and husks) and lets the heavy grain (seeds) fall to the ground. The grain is collected and put into sacks.

When school is out, Assim sometimes goes down to the mill to watch
the miller at work. The miller is proud
of the oil engine that turns the big
grindstone. It is new and was made
in Pakistan.

When the engine is working, its
familiar "woop, woop" sound can be
heard all over the village. This sound
tells the villagers that the miller is at
work and will grind their sacks of
flour for them.

Assim likes to go into Rawalpindi with his father to buy things from the market. They often take the bus, which gets very crowded.

The rack on the roof of this bus was built to carry luggage, but the bus is so full that people have climbed up on top to sit on it. In large cities, the police do not allow passengers to ride on the roof of the bus.

Many people also travel by bicycle or in *tongas*, which are horse-drawn carts.

Rawalpindi is a very busy city, and the fourth largest city in Pakistan. Many signs and advertisements are written in both Urdu and English. Although Urdu is the official language of Pakistan, most people speak the language of their area. Assim's family speaks Punjabi because they live in the Punjab.

Some of the Pakistani men dress in western style clothing and wear shirts, ties, and sport coats. Others dress Pakistani style, wearing shirts and *shalwar*.

The water seller is kept busy supplying water to the city shopkeepers. His skin bag is a buffalo hide. He fills his bag from a faucet on the street.

The stores and stalls in the market sell many different kinds of things, including food, clothing, furniture, and jewelry.

This fruit stand has apples, oranges, bananas, guavas, and sweet juicy *kainos*, which look like large tangerines and are only grown in Pakistan.

Assim's father likes to buy fruit for the family. In the summer he brings home melons and mangoes.

At another stall, a man cuts long sticks of sugar cane into small pieces which people chew for the juice. The large block of ice on top of the pieces of sugar cane keeps them cool.

This stall sells salt and spices —chilies and *haldi*. Pakistanis enjoy spicy foods and meat is often prepared with a spicy sauce and eaten with rice. Spices are also used when making kebabs, which are pieces of meat usually cooked on skewers over a charcoal fire.

Assim likes to stop at the sweets stall. Delicacies like those shown here are only served on festive occasions, like weddings and parties.

When he has time, Assim stops to watch the craftsmen at work in the market. Some make colorful pottery or hammer beautiful patterns on copper bowls and plates. Others make very fine gold and silver jewelry.

This man is making a *charpoy*, a piece of furniture used indoors as a bed and outside as a couch to rest on. The *charpoy* is made with jute string or strips of leather. A gap is left at one end and laced with strings. If the webbing sags, the strings can be tightened.

One of the streets near the market is decorated for a wedding. All the relatives and friends of the bride and bridegroom have joined together to celebrate the occasion.

The bride wears a beautifully embroidered red *gharara*, or veil, and a golden shawl. Her necklaces, bracelets, rings, and head ornaments are all made of pure gold. The bridegroom wears garlands of money given to him by his relatives. The bride's family has provided everything that the bride will need in her new home.

One day, Assim and his father go to a festival in a nearby village. The festival is a competition between pairs of oxen yoked to the wheel of the well.

The blindfolded oxen race around and around the well in a circle. The winners are the pair that can race around the well the most often in ten minutes.

While the animals run, fireworks are set off and musicians play drums, bagpipes, and trumpets.

A large crowd of people has gathered to watch the competition. Seven pairs of oxen are in the contest. The midday sun is very hot, and many spectators stand in the shade of a mango tree.

The judges for the competition announce the winners, and the crowd cheers. This pair of oxen has races around the well 145 times in ten minutes! They are decorated and their owner receives a prize.

In his geography lessons at school, Assim has learned about the Tarbela Dam on the Indus River, about 60 miles (100 kilometers) from Rawalpindi.

The dam was completed in 1976 and is the largest rock and earth filled dam in the world. It helps produce electricity for factories, offices, shops, and houses. The water it supplies irrigates the land, and the farmers are able to grow more crops.

Before construction could begin on the dam, though, many people had to move. They were living on land that would be under water as soon as the dam was built.

The Awami express train stops at the Rawalpindi railroad station on its way from Peshawar, in northern Pakistan, to Karachi, a large city in the south.

Sometimes during his summer vacation, Assim takes the train from Rawalpindi to Lyallpur to visit his uncle. Lyallpur is an even larger city than Rawalpindi.

The trip takes almost a day. At each stop along the way, passengers are able to buy food and beverages from carts on the station platform.

Assim's uncle works at one of the big textile, or cloth, mills in Lyallpur. The making of cotton cloth is Pakistan's leading industry.

Assim loves to tour the mill with his uncle. He is fascinated by the large looms that embroider intricate patterns on colored nylon cloth. Most of the cloth woven in the mill, though, is cotton. Pakistan grows a lot of cotton.

With so much to see and do, Assim's week in Lyallpur passes very quickly. Soon it's time to board the train for home. Already Assim has decided that he would like to visit again next summer.

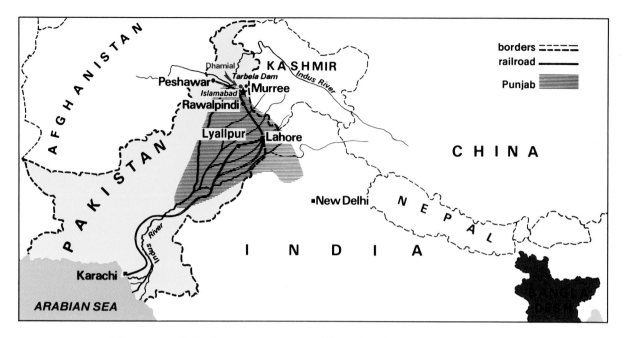

The word Pakistan means "land of the pure" in Urdu. The country was named that by the Muslim people who worked to create the nation.

Pakistan is still a very young country. The land that is now called Pakistan was for centuries part of India. When Great Britain granted independence to India in 1947, the country was divided up according to religious beliefs. Two areas were sectioned off, one on each side of the country; they were named East Pakistan and West Pakistan. Most of the people who lived in East and West Pakistan were Muslims, like Assim's family. The people who lived in the central area, which was still called India, were Hindus.

In 1971, war broke out between East Pakistan and West Pakistan. East Pakistan declared itself an independent country and is known today as Bangladesh.

Facts about Pakistan

Official Name: The Islamic Republic of Pakistan

Capital: Islamabad

Official Language: Urdu

Form of Money: Pakistani rupee

Area: 310,404 square miles (803,943 square kilometers)
  The United States is about 10 times bigger than Pakistan.

Population: about 91 million people
  The United States has about 2½ times as many people as Pakistan.

NORTH
AMERICA

SOUTH
AMERICA

EUROPE

A S I A

Pakistan

AFRICA

AUSTRALIA

Families the World Over

Some children in foreign countries live like you do. Others live very differently. In these books, you can meet children from all over the world. You'll learn about their games and schools, their families and friends, and what it's like to grow up in a faraway land.

A FAMILY IN CHINA   A FAMILY IN PAKISTAN   A FAMILY IN BRAZIL
A FAMILY IN EGYPT   A FAMILY IN SRI LANKA   A FAMILY IN CHILE
A FAMILY IN FRANCE   A FAMILY IN WEST GERMANY   A FAMILY IN IRELAND
A FAMILY IN INDIA   AN ABORIGINAL FAMILY   A FAMILY IN MOROCCO
A FAMILY IN JAMAICA   AN ARAB FAMILY   A FAMILY IN SINGAPORE
A FAMILY IN NIGERIA   AN ESKIMO FAMILY   A ZULU FAMILY

Lerner Publications Company
241 First Avenue North
Minneapolis, Minnesota 55401